Fiction
at this level

FISHING FOR
TROUBLE
DAVID and HELEN ORME

978 1 4451 1812 3 pb

FOOTBALL
LEGEND
DAVID and HELEN ORME

978 1 4451 1811 6 pb

VAMPIRES ARE
SO BORING
DAVID and HELEN ORME

978 1 4451 1813 0 pb

MY NAME IS
COLEN
STEVE BARLOW and STEVE SKIDMORE

978 1 4451 3070 5 pb

DEVIL'S
TEETH
STEVE BARLOW and STEVE SKIDMORE

978 1 4451 3054 5 pb

SPACE
STATION ALERT
DAVID and HELEN ORME

978 1 4451 3068 2 pb

Graphic fiction
at this level

DEMON
STREAK
JONNY ZUCKER and STEVE SAMPSON

978 1 4451 1799 7 pb

FULL METAL
HERO
JONNY ZUCKER and DAN BOULTWOOD

978 1 4451 1801 7 pb

TERROR
BEAST
JONNY ZUCKER and MACK CHATER

978 1 4451 1800 0 pb

ALIEN
ACADEMY
JONNY ZUCKER and RYAN PENTNEY

978 1 4451 3088 0 pb

DOWNHILL
RACERS
JONNY ZUCKER and IAIN BUCHANAN

978 1 4451 3089 7 pb

BEYOND THE
WALL
JONNY ZUCKER and TOMAS ARANDA

978 1 4451 3090 3 pb

Non-fiction
at this level

BIZARRE
BUILDINGS
ANNE ROONEY

978 1 4451 1952 6 hb
978 1 4451 3229 7 pb

CRAZY
FOOD
ANNE ROONEY

978 1 4451 1954 0 hb
978 1 4451 3228 0 pb

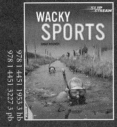

WACKY
SPORTS
ANNE ROONEY

978 1 4451 1953 3 hb
978 1 4451 3227 3 pb

AMAZING
PETS
ANNE ROONEY

978 1 4451 3050 7 hb

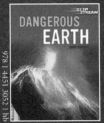

DANGEROUS
EARTH
ANNE ROONEY

978 1 4451 3052 1 hb

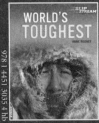

WORLD'S
TOUGHEST
ANNE ROONEY

978 1 4451 3035 4 hb

SLIP STREAM

AMAZING PETS

ANNE ROONEY

EDGE
FRANKLIN
WATTS

LONDON · SYDNEY

First published in 2014 by
Franklin Watts
338 Euston Road
London NW1 3BH

Franklin Watts Australia
Level 17/207 Kent Street
Sydney NSW 2000

© Franklin Watts 2014

(hb) ISBN: 978 1 4451 3050 7
(Library ebook) ISBN: 978 1 4451 3051 4

Dewey classification number: 636'.0887

The right of Anne Rooney to be
identified as the author of this Work
has been asserted in accordance
with the Copyright, Designs and
Patents Act, 1988.

A CIP catalogue record for this book
is available from the British Library.

Series Editors: Adrian Cole and Jackie Hamley
Series Advisors: Diana Bentley and Dee Reid
Series Designer: Peter Scoulding
Designer: Cathryn Gilbert
Picture Researcher: Diana Morris

Printed in China

Franklin Watts is a division of
Hachette Children's Books,
an Hachette UK company.
www.hachette.co.uk

Acknowledgements:
Carlo Allegri/Getty Images: 8.
John Audrey/istockphoto: 15.
aureapterus/istockphoto: 16.
Shawn Baldwin/AP/PAI: 22.
Barcroft Media/Getty Images: 1, 20.
Andrew Burgess/istockphoto: 17.
David Callan/istockphoto: 12.
Caters News Agency: front cover, 4cr, 6.
Johannes Compann/istockphoto: 21.
froxx/istockphoto: 4-5b.
David Garry/Getty Images: 13.
Patric Habans/Paris Match/Getty Images: 9.
Sean Lima/Shutterstock: 19.
Thierry Maffeis/Dreamstime: 14.
Marti157500/Dreamstime: 5, 23.
Mik122/istockphoto: 11.
Potnc/Dreamstime: 4cl, 18.
sqback/istockphoto: 7.
Roman Zaremba/Dreamstime: 10.

Every attempt has been made to
clear copyright. Should there be any
inadvertent omission, please apply
to the publisher for rectification.

CONTENTS

COOL PETS!

Some people keep amazing pets!
Which pet do you think is the coolest?

CLEVER!

Arbor is a rescue dog. Her owners
found she was good at painting.

Some of her pictures sell for lots of money — one sold for £600!

WACKY!

A buffalo is a huge pet! This one is called Bailey Junior.

The painter
Salvador Dalí
kept an anteater.
He took it for
walks in Paris.
Then he drew it
in some of his
paintings.

GREEDY!

Piranhas are fierce fish from South America. Some people keep them in fish tanks. Piranhas eat meat. If you get some, don't dip your fingers in the water!

35

36 ▶

NEGATIVE 35 mm

CUTE!

This is a sugar glider. It is a small possum that can fly! It glides using flaps of skin between its hands and feet.

36

35

NEGATIVE 35 mm.

Sugar gliders are cute, but you need to buy live bugs for them to eat.

CREEPY!

Tarantulas are giant spiders. Their bite is poisonous.
If a tarantula bites you it will hurt, but it won't kill you.

You will have to feed a tarantula live insects and even baby mice.

FREAKY!

Axlotls (say ax-oh-lot-uls) come from Mexico. They need to be kept in a tank of water.

If an axlotl loses an arm or a leg, it can grow a new one!

SLIMY!

A giant African land snail is very big and smelly.
It eats leaves and vegetables.

A banana slug is bright yellow.
They are easy to keep, but
would you like one?

OVERGROWN!

This capybara looks like a giant guinea pig. A couple in Texas, USA, have him as a pet.

HEROIC!

Lulu the pig stopped a car. She brought
the driver to her owner, who was ill.

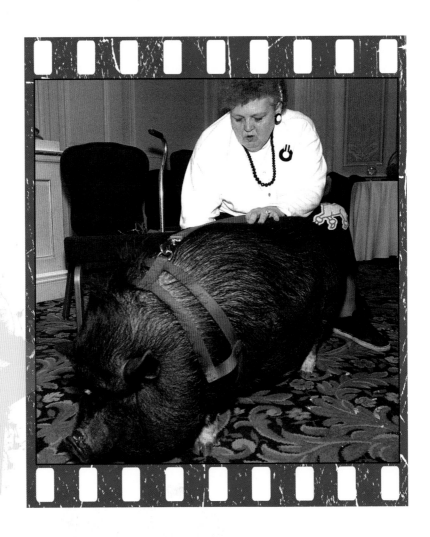

Willie the parrot saved a choking child. He shouted "Mama, baby!" until the baby-sitter noticed.

Which amazing pet would you choose?

23

INDEX

FOR TEACHERS

About

SLIP STREAM

Slipstream is a series of expertly levelled books designed for pupils who are struggling with reading. Its unique three-strand approach through fiction, graphic fiction and non-fiction gives pupils a rich reading experience that will accelerate their progress and close the reading gap.

At the heart of every Slipstream non-fiction book is exciting information. Easily accessible words and phrases ensure that pupils both decode and comprehend, and the topics really engage older struggling readers.

Whether you're using Slipstream Level 2 for Guided Reading or as an independent read, here are some suggestions:

1. Make each reading session successful. Talk about the text before the pupil starts reading. Introduce any unfamiliar vocabulary.

2. Encourage the pupil to talk about the book using a range of open questions. For example, which amazing pet would they most like? Why?

3. Discuss the differences between reading non-fiction, fiction and graphic fiction. Which do they prefer?

For guidance, SLIPSTREAM Level 2 – Amazing Pets has been approximately measured to:

National Curriculum Level: 2b
Reading Age: 7.6–8.0
Book Band: Purple

ATOS: 2.1*
Guided Reading Level: I
Lexile® Measure (confirmed): 520L

*Please check actual Accelerated Reader™ book level and quiz availability at www.arbookfind.co.uk